Thi

journal belongs to

Date started

First published by Oh My Days Publishing, London, 2020

CONTENTS

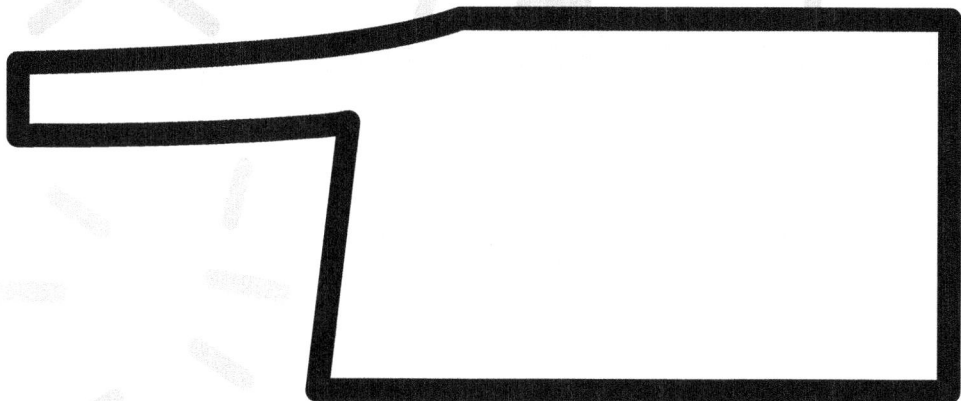

WHAT DOES GROWTH MINDSET MEAN?

What does growth mindset mean?

Your mindset is the way you think about and approach challenges in life.

Growth mindset is a positive and productive way of thinking. People with a growth mindset believe that brains and talent are just a starting point and that with dedication and hard work they can accomplish great things.

The opposite to a growth mindset is a 'fixed mindset'. People with a fixed mindset say things like "I'm not an artist".

People with a growth mindset would say "with practice, dedication, hard work and time I'll create a masterpiece".

Getting up and trying again

Grow mindset people think that mistakes are good. They believe that nothing great ever happens on the first attempt. Getting it wrong and making mistakes is the best way to learn. It makes you think about solutions and new ideas.

"I've missed more than 9000 shots in my career. I've lost almost 300 games. 26 times, I've been trusted to take the game winning shot and missed. I've failed over and over and over again in my life. And that is why I succeed."

Michael Jordan

Here's the science...

Your brain is a bit like a muscle the more you exercise it the stronger and faster it gets!

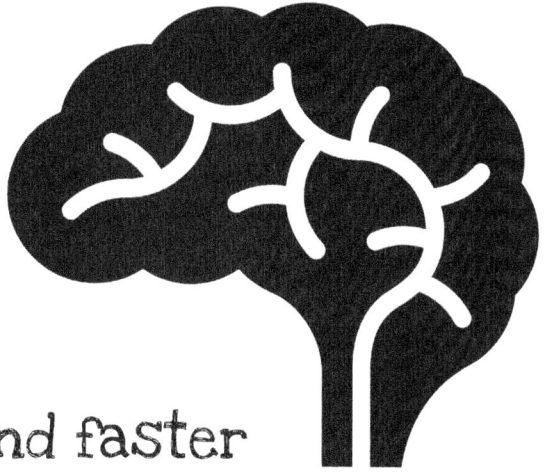

It is full of tiny things called neurons, you have nearly 100 billion of them! These are the things that do all of the work.

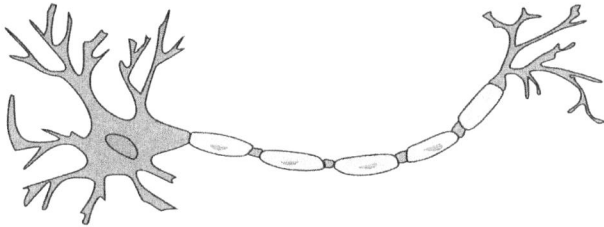

They send and receive information along connections. The more you do something the stronger these connections become and the faster the information can travel.

2

PERSONAL INFO

?

What are your
strengths?

What would you
like to improve?

List people who
inspire you:

List people who help
you:

Write something about your greatest achievement ever.

Write about the
biggest lesson you ever
learned from making a mistake.

Share something that you found really difficult at first but persevered with.

3

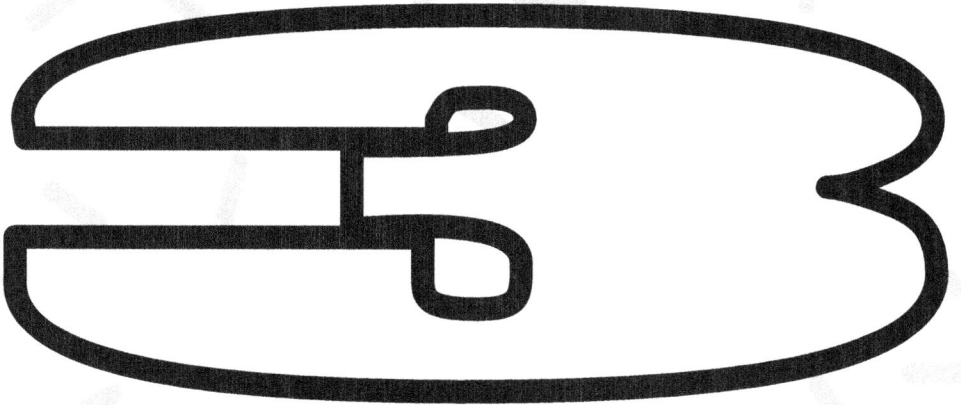

HOW TO USE THIS JOURNAL

It's good to notice positive things. Note the most positive thing that you have experienced in the last 24 hours.

Tick all that apply. Think about doing as many as you can every day.

Date

Growth Mindset Journal

Most positive thing.

CHECKLIST

FELT INSPIRED ☐
ACHIEVED SOMETHING ☐
MADE A MISTAKE ☐
LEARNT SOMETHING NEW ☐
DID A DIFFICULT THING ☐
TRIED SOMETHING NEW ☐
HELPED SOMEONE ☐
SOMEONE HELPED ME ☐
FELT PROUD ☐
SURPRISED MYSELF ☐
TRIED MY BEST ☐
STAYED FOCUSED ☐
IMPROVED A SKILL ☐
PERSONAL BEST ☐
ENJOYED A CHALLENGE ☐
REACHED A GOAL ☐
SET A NEW GOAL ☐
SOLVED A PROBLEM ☐

A challenge you faced.

Say a negative thing in a positive way.

Remember, growth mindset people make positives out of negatives!

Challenges help us grow. Think of a challenge however big or small.

Mistakes are good! Think about a mistake you have made in the last 24 hours.

How did you learn from your mistake? What would you do differently next time?

A mistake you made.	What you learned from that mistake.
Set a goal, however big or small.	**MINDSET-O-METER** FIXED GROWTH

Think about something you'd like to do, learn or achieve.

Draw the needle to rate your mindset for the last 24 hours. Has it been a fixed mindset (I can't) or a growth mindset (I can if I try) kind of day?

4 JOURNAL

Growth Mindset Journal

Date: 5/6/20

Most positive thing.

Achieved something

A challenge you faced.

Not stepping on the elastic

Say a negative thing in a positive way.

I can't do it yet

CHECKLIST

FELT INSPIRED	☑
ACHIEVED SOMETHING	☐
MADE A MISTAKE	☐
LEARNT SOMETHING NEW	☐
DID A DIFFICULT THING	☐
TRIED SOMETHING NEW	☐
HELPED SOMEONE	☐
SOMEONE HELPED ME	☐
FELT PROUD	☐
SURPRISED MYSELF	☐
TRIED MY BEST	☐
STAYED FOCUSED	☐
IMPROVED A SKILL	☐
PERSONAL BEST	☐
ENJOYED A CHALLENGE	☐
REACHED A GOAL	☐
SET A NEW GOAL	☐
SOLVED A PROBLEM	☐

A mistake you made.

Treading on the elastic

What you learned from that mistake.

keep practising

Set a goal, however big or small.

Doing it twice without treading on the elastic

MINDSET-O-METER

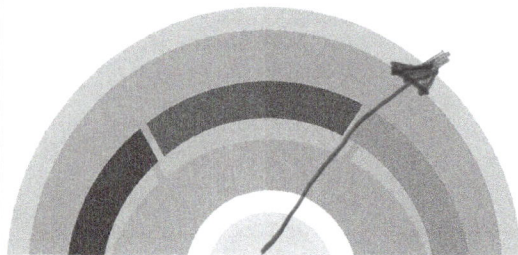

FIXED   GROWTH

Growth Mindset Journal

Most positive thing.

CHECKLIST

FELT INSPIRED	☐
ACHIEVED SOMETHING	☐
MADE A MISTAKE	☐
LEARNT SOMETHING NEW	☐
DID A DIFFICULT THING	☐
TRIED SOMETHING NEW	☐
HELPED SOMEONE	☐
SOMEONE HELPED ME	☐
FELT PROUD	☐
SURPRISED MYSELF	☐
TRIED MY BEST	☐
STAYED FOCUSED	☐
IMPROVED A SKILL	☐
PERSONAL BEST	☐
ENJOYED A CHALLENGE	☐
REACHED A GOAL	☐
SET A NEW GOAL	☐
SOLVED A PROBLEM	☐

A challenge you faced.

Say a negative thing in a positive way.

A mistake you made.

What you learned from that mistake.

Set a goal, however big or small.

MINDSET-O-METER

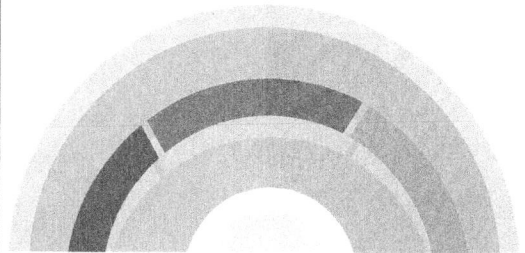

FIXED   GROWTH

Date:

Growth Mindset Journal

Most positive thing.

CHECKLIST

FELT INSPIRED ☐
ACHIEVED SOMETHING ☐
MADE A MISTAKE ☐
LEARNT SOMETHING NEW ☐
DID A DIFFICULT THING ☐
TRIED SOMETHING NEW ☐
HELPED SOMEONE ☐
SOMEONE HELPED ME ☐
FELT PROUD ☐
SURPRISED MYSELF ☐
TRIED MY BEST ☐
STAYED FOCUSED ☐
IMPROVED A SKILL ☐
PERSONAL BEST ☐
ENJOYED A CHALLENGE ☐
REACHED A GOAL ☐
SET A NEW GOAL ☐
SOLVED A PROBLEM ☐

A challenge you faced.

Say a negative thing in a positive way.

A mistake you made.

What you learned from that mistake.

Set a goal, however big or small.

MINDSET-O-METER

FIXED   GROWTH

Date:

Growth Mindset Journal

Most positive thing.

CHECKLIST

FELT INSPIRED	☐
ACHIEVED SOMETHING	☐
MADE A MISTAKE	☐
LEARNT SOMETHING NEW	☐
DID A DIFFICULT THING	☐
TRIED SOMETHING NEW	☐
HELPED SOMEONE	☐
SOMEONE HELPED ME	☐
FELT PROUD	☐
SURPRISED MYSELF	☐
TRIED MY BEST	☐
STAYED FOCUSED	☐
IMPROVED A SKILL	☐
PERSONAL BEST	☐
ENJOYED A CHALLENGE	☐
REACHED A GOAL	☐
SET A NEW GOAL	☐
SOLVED A PROBLEM	☐

A challenge you faced.

Say a negative thing in a positive way.

A mistake you made.

What you learned from that mistake.

Set a goal, however big or small.

MINDSET-O-METER

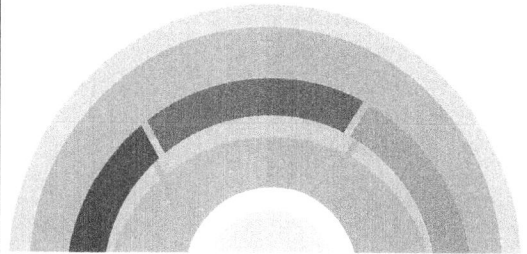

FIXED   GROWTH

Date:

Growth Mindset Journal

Most positive thing.

CHECKLIST

FELT INSPIRED	☐
ACHIEVED SOMETHING	☐
MADE A MISTAKE	☐
LEARNT SOMETHING NEW	☐
DID A DIFFICULT THING	☐
TRIED SOMETHING NEW	☐
HELPED SOMEONE	☐
SOMEONE HELPED ME	☐
FELT PROUD	☐
SURPRISED MYSELF	☐
TRIED MY BEST	☐
STAYED FOCUSED	☐
IMPROVED A SKILL	☐
PERSONAL BEST	☐
ENJOYED A CHALLENGE	☐
REACHED A GOAL	☐
SET A NEW GOAL	☐
SOLVED A PROBLEM	☐

A challenge you faced.

Say a negative thing in a positive way.

A mistake you made.

What you learned from that mistake.

Set a goal, however big or small.

MINDSET-O-METER

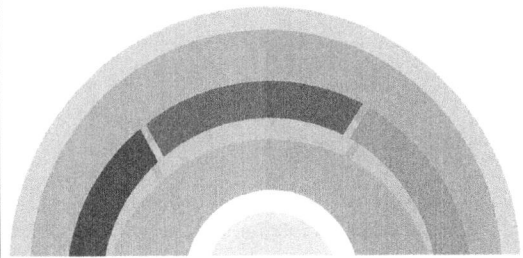

FIXED   GROWTH

Date:

Growth Mindset Journal

Most positive thing.

CHECKLIST

FELT INSPIRED ☐
ACHIEVED SOMETHING ☐
MADE A MISTAKE ☐
LEARNT SOMETHING NEW ☐
DID A DIFFICULT THING ☐
TRIED SOMETHING NEW ☐
HELPED SOMEONE ☐
SOMEONE HELPED ME ☐
FELT PROUD ☐
SURPRISED MYSELF ☐
TRIED MY BEST ☐
STAYED FOCUSED ☐
IMPROVED A SKILL ☐
PERSONAL BEST ☐
ENJOYED A CHALLENGE ☐
REACHED A GOAL ☐
SET A NEW GOAL ☐
SOLVED A PROBLEM ☐

A challenge you faced.

Say a negative thing in a positive way.

A mistake you made.

What you learned from that mistake.

Set a goal, however big or small.

MINDSET-O-METER

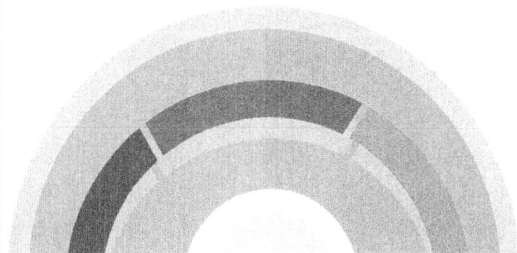

FIXED   GROWTH

Growth Mindset Journal

Most positive thing.

CHECKLIST

FELT INSPIRED	☐
ACHIEVED SOMETHING	☐
MADE A MISTAKE	☐
LEARNT SOMETHING NEW	☐
DID A DIFFICULT THING	☐
TRIED SOMETHING NEW	☐
HELPED SOMEONE	☐
SOMEONE HELPED ME	☐
FELT PROUD	☐
SURPRISED MYSELF	☐
TRIED MY BEST	☐
STAYED FOCUSED	☐
IMPROVED A SKILL	☐
PERSONAL BEST	☐
ENJOYED A CHALLENGE	☐
REACHED A GOAL	☐
SET A NEW GOAL	☐
SOLVED A PROBLEM	☐

A challenge you faced.

Say a negative thing in a positive way.

A mistake you made.

What you learned from that mistake.

Set a goal, however big or small.

MINDSET-O-METER

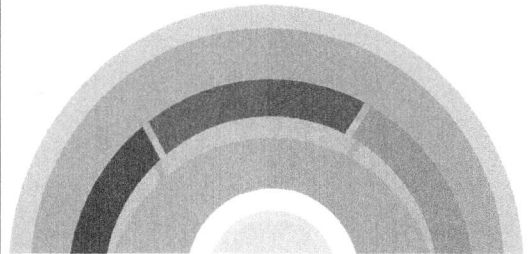

FIXED　　　　　　　　　GROWTH

Growth Mindset Journal

Most positive thing.

CHECKLIST

FELT INSPIRED	☐
ACHIEVED SOMETHING	☐
MADE A MISTAKE	☐
LEARNT SOMETHING NEW	☐
DID A DIFFICULT THING	☐
TRIED SOMETHING NEW	☐
HELPED SOMEONE	☐
SOMEONE HELPED ME	☐
FELT PROUD	☐
SURPRISED MYSELF	☐
TRIED MY BEST	☐
STAYED FOCUSED	☐
IMPROVED A SKILL	☐
PERSONAL BEST	☐
ENJOYED A CHALLENGE	☐
REACHED A GOAL	☐
SET A NEW GOAL	☐
SOLVED A PROBLEM	☐

A challenge you faced.

Say a negative thing in a positive way.

A mistake you made.

What you learned from that mistake.

Set a goal, however big or small.

MINDSET-O-METER

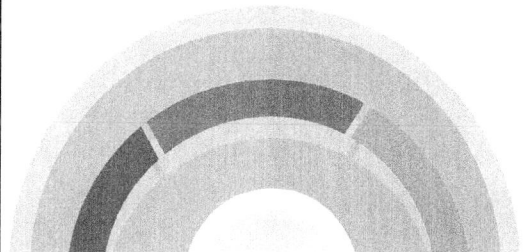

FIXED   GROWTH

Growth Mindset Journal

Most positive thing.

CHECKLIST

FELT INSPIRED	☐
ACHIEVED SOMETHING	☐
MADE A MISTAKE	☐
LEARNT SOMETHING NEW	☐
DID A DIFFICULT THING	☐
TRIED SOMETHING NEW	☐
HELPED SOMEONE	☐
SOMEONE HELPED ME	☐
FELT PROUD	☐
SURPRISED MYSELF	☐
TRIED MY BEST	☐
STAYED FOCUSED	☐
IMPROVED A SKILL	☐
PERSONAL BEST	☐
ENJOYED A CHALLENGE	☐
REACHED A GOAL	☐
SET A NEW GOAL	☐
SOLVED A PROBLEM	☐

A challenge you faced.

Say a negative thing in a positive way.

A mistake you made.

What you learned from that mistake.

Set a goal, however big or small.

MINDSET-O-METER

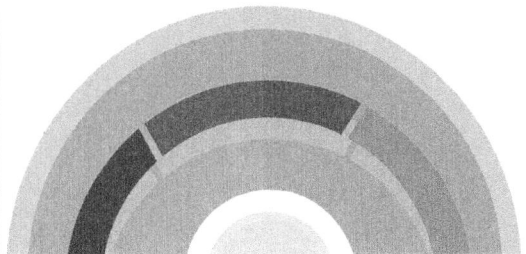

FIXED   GROWTH

Growth Mindset Journal

Most positive thing.

CHECKLIST

FELT INSPIRED ☐
ACHIEVED SOMETHING ☐
MADE A MISTAKE ☐
LEARNT SOMETHING NEW ☐
DID A DIFFICULT THING ☐
TRIED SOMETHING NEW ☐
HELPED SOMEONE ☐
SOMEONE HELPED ME ☐
FELT PROUD ☐
SURPRISED MYSELF ☐
TRIED MY BEST ☐
STAYED FOCUSED ☐
IMPROVED A SKILL ☐
PERSONAL BEST ☐
ENJOYED A CHALLENGE ☐
REACHED A GOAL ☐
SET A NEW GOAL ☐
SOLVED A PROBLEM ☐

A challenge you faced.

Say a negative thing in a positive way.

A mistake you made.

What you learned from that mistake.

Set a goal, however big or small.

MINDSET-O-METER

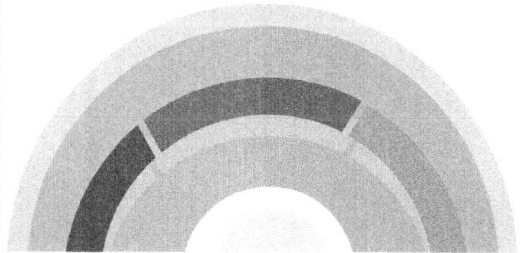

FIXED   GROWTH

Growth Mindset Journal

Most positive thing.

CHECKLIST

FELT INSPIRED ☐
ACHIEVED SOMETHING ☐
MADE A MISTAKE ☐
LEARNT SOMETHING NEW ☐
DID A DIFFICULT THING ☐
TRIED SOMETHING NEW ☐
HELPED SOMEONE ☐
SOMEONE HELPED ME ☐
FELT PROUD ☐
SURPRISED MYSELF ☐
TRIED MY BEST ☐
STAYED FOCUSED ☐
IMPROVED A SKILL ☐
PERSONAL BEST ☐
ENJOYED A CHALLENGE ☐
REACHED A GOAL ☐
SET A NEW GOAL ☐
SOLVED A PROBLEM ☐

A challenge you faced.

Say a negative thing in a positive way.

A mistake you made.

What you learned from that mistake.

Set a goal, however big or small.

MINDSET-O-METER

FIXED   GROWTH

Date:

Growth Mindset Journal

Most positive thing.

CHECKLIST

FELT INSPIRED	☐
ACHIEVED SOMETHING	☐
MADE A MISTAKE	☐
LEARNT SOMETHING NEW	☐
DID A DIFFICULT THING	☐
TRIED SOMETHING NEW	☐
HELPED SOMEONE	☐
SOMEONE HELPED ME	☐
FELT PROUD	☐
SURPRISED MYSELF	☐
TRIED MY BEST	☐
STAYED FOCUSED	☐
IMPROVED A SKILL	☐
PERSONAL BEST	☐
ENJOYED A CHALLENGE	☐
REACHED A GOAL	☐
SET A NEW GOAL	☐
SOLVED A PROBLEM	☐

A challenge you faced.

Say a negative thing in a positive way.

A mistake you made.

What you learned from that mistake.

Set a goal, however big or small.

MINDSET-O-METER

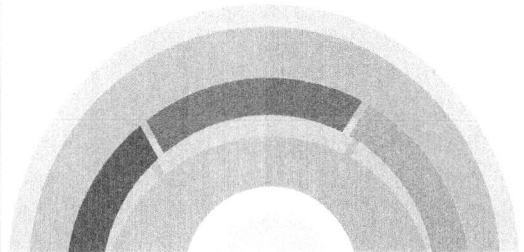

FIXED   GROWTH

Growth Mindset Journal

Most positive thing.

CHECKLIST

FELT INSPIRED ☐
ACHIEVED SOMETHING ☐
MADE A MISTAKE ☐
LEARNT SOMETHING NEW ☐
DID A DIFFICULT THING ☐
TRIED SOMETHING NEW ☐
HELPED SOMEONE ☐
SOMEONE HELPED ME ☐
FELT PROUD ☐
SURPRISED MYSELF ☐
TRIED MY BEST ☐
STAYED FOCUSED ☐
IMPROVED A SKILL ☐
PERSONAL BEST ☐
ENJOYED A CHALLENGE ☐
REACHED A GOAL ☐
SET A NEW GOAL ☐
SOLVED A PROBLEM ☐

A challenge you faced.

Say a negative thing in a positive way.

A mistake you made.

What you learned from that mistake.

Set a goal, however big or small.

MINDSET-O-METER

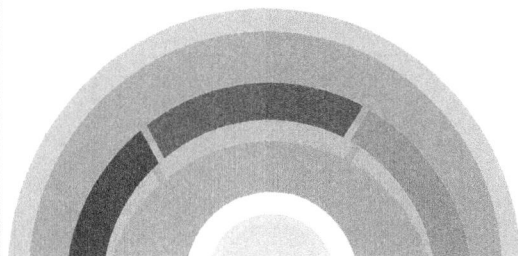

FIXED   GROWTH

Date:

Growth Mindset Journal

Most positive thing.

CHECKLIST

FELT INSPIRED	☐
ACHIEVED SOMETHING	☐
MADE A MISTAKE	☐
LEARNT SOMETHING NEW	☐
DID A DIFFICULT THING	☐
TRIED SOMETHING NEW	☐
HELPED SOMEONE	☐
SOMEONE HELPED ME	☐
FELT PROUD	☐
SURPRISED MYSELF	☐
TRIED MY BEST	☐
STAYED FOCUSED	☐
IMPROVED A SKILL	☐
PERSONAL BEST	☐
ENJOYED A CHALLENGE	☐
REACHED A GOAL	☐
SET A NEW GOAL	☐
SOLVED A PROBLEM	☐

A challenge you faced.

Say a negative thing in a positive way.

A mistake you made.

What you learned from that mistake.

Set a goal, however big or small.

MINDSET-O-METER

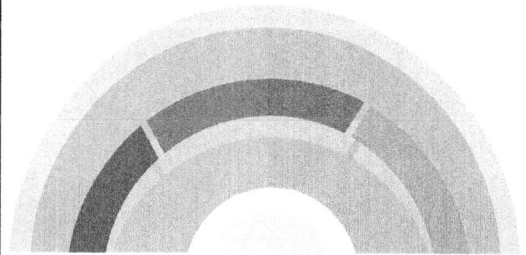

FIXED   GROWTH

Growth Mindset Journal

Most positive thing.

CHECKLIST

FELT INSPIRED	☐
ACHIEVED SOMETHING	☐
MADE A MISTAKE	☐
LEARNT SOMETHING NEW	☐
DID A DIFFICULT THING	☐
TRIED SOMETHING NEW	☐
HELPED SOMEONE	☐
SOMEONE HELPED ME	☐
FELT PROUD	☐
SURPRISED MYSELF	☐
TRIED MY BEST	☐
STAYED FOCUSED	☐
IMPROVED A SKILL	☐
PERSONAL BEST	☐
ENJOYED A CHALLENGE	☐
REACHED A GOAL	☐
SET A NEW GOAL	☐
SOLVED A PROBLEM	☐

A challenge you faced.

Say a negative thing in a positive way.

A mistake you made.

What you learned from that mistake.

Set a goal, however big or small.

MINDSET-O-METER

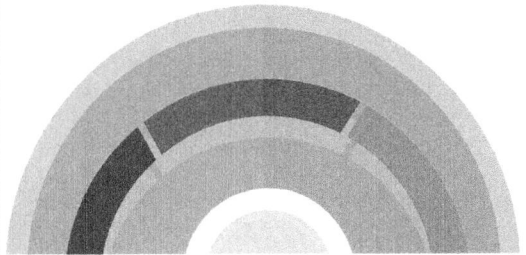

FIXED   GROWTH

Date:

Growth Mindset Journal

Most positive thing.

CHECKLIST

FELT INSPIRED ☐
ACHIEVED SOMETHING ☐
MADE A MISTAKE ☐
LEARNT SOMETHING NEW ☐
DID A DIFFICULT THING ☐
TRIED SOMETHING NEW ☐
HELPED SOMEONE ☐
SOMEONE HELPED ME ☐
FELT PROUD ☐
SURPRISED MYSELF ☐
TRIED MY BEST ☐
STAYED FOCUSED ☐
IMPROVED A SKILL ☐
PERSONAL BEST ☐
ENJOYED A CHALLENGE ☐
REACHED A GOAL ☐
SET A NEW GOAL ☐
SOLVED A PROBLEM ☐

A challenge you faced.

Say a negative thing in a positive way.

A mistake you made.

What you learned from that mistake.

Set a goal, however big or small.

MINDSET-O-METER

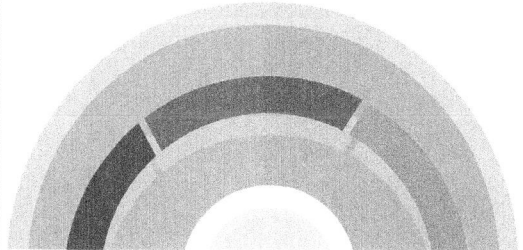

FIXED   GROWTH

Growth Mindset Journal

Most positive thing.

CHECKLIST

FELT INSPIRED	☐
ACHIEVED SOMETHING	☐
MADE A MISTAKE	☐
LEARNT SOMETHING NEW	☐
DID A DIFFICULT THING	☐
TRIED SOMETHING NEW	☐
HELPED SOMEONE	☐
SOMEONE HELPED ME	☐
FELT PROUD	☐
SURPRISED MYSELF	☐
TRIED MY BEST	☐
STAYED FOCUSED	☐
IMPROVED A SKILL	☐
PERSONAL BEST	☐
ENJOYED A CHALLENGE	☐
REACHED A GOAL	☐
SET A NEW GOAL	☐
SOLVED A PROBLEM	☐

A challenge you faced.

Say a negative thing in a positive way.

A mistake you made.

What you learned from that mistake.

Set a goal, however big or small.

MINDSET-O-METER

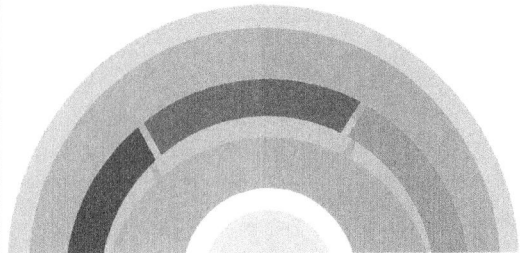

FIXED   GROWTH

Growth Mindset Journal

Most positive thing.

CHECKLIST

FELT INSPIRED ☐
ACHIEVED SOMETHING ☐
MADE A MISTAKE ☐
LEARNT SOMETHING NEW ☐
DID A DIFFICULT THING ☐
TRIED SOMETHING NEW ☐
HELPED SOMEONE ☐
SOMEONE HELPED ME ☐
FELT PROUD ☐
SURPRISED MYSELF ☐
TRIED MY BEST ☐
STAYED FOCUSED ☐
IMPROVED A SKILL ☐
PERSONAL BEST ☐
ENJOYED A CHALLENGE ☐
REACHED A GOAL ☐
SET A NEW GOAL ☐
SOLVED A PROBLEM ☐

A challenge you faced.

Say a negative thing in a positive way.

A mistake you made.

What you learned from that mistake.

Set a goal, however big or small.

MINDSET-O-METER

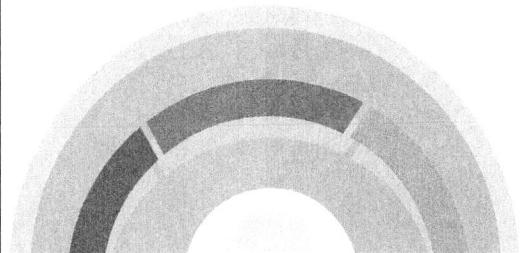

FIXED   GROWTH

Growth Mindset Journal

Most positive thing.

CHECKLIST

FELT INSPIRED	☐
ACHIEVED SOMETHING	☐
MADE A MISTAKE	☐
LEARNT SOMETHING NEW	☐
DID A DIFFICULT THING	☐
TRIED SOMETHING NEW	☐
HELPED SOMEONE	☐
SOMEONE HELPED ME	☐
FELT PROUD	☐
SURPRISED MYSELF	☐
TRIED MY BEST	☐
STAYED FOCUSED	☐
IMPROVED A SKILL	☐
PERSONAL BEST	☐
ENJOYED A CHALLENGE	☐
REACHED A GOAL	☐
SET A NEW GOAL	☐
SOLVED A PROBLEM	☐

A challenge you faced.

Say a negative thing in a positive way.

A mistake you made.

What you learned from that mistake.

Set a goal, however big or small.

MINDSET-O-METER

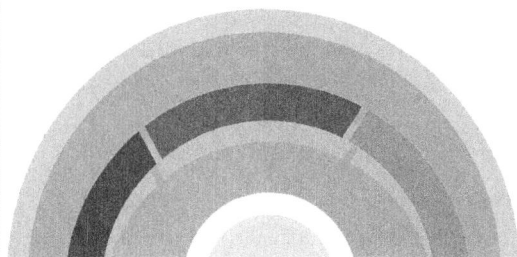

FIXED   GROWTH

Date:

Growth Mindset Journal

Most positive thing.

CHECKLIST

FELT INSPIRED ☐
ACHIEVED SOMETHING ☐
MADE A MISTAKE ☐
LEARNT SOMETHING NEW ☐
DID A DIFFICULT THING ☐
TRIED SOMETHING NEW ☐
HELPED SOMEONE ☐
SOMEONE HELPED ME ☐
FELT PROUD ☐
SURPRISED MYSELF ☐
TRIED MY BEST ☐
STAYED FOCUSED ☐
IMPROVED A SKILL ☐
PERSONAL BEST ☐
ENJOYED A CHALLENGE ☐
REACHED A GOAL ☐
SET A NEW GOAL ☐
SOLVED A PROBLEM ☐

A challenge you faced.

Say a negative thing in a positive way.

A mistake you made.

What you learned from that mistake.

Set a goal, however big or small.

MINDSET-O-METER

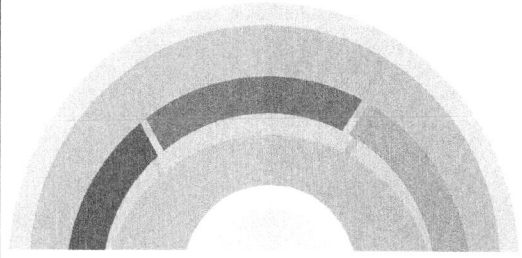

FIXED · GROWTH

Date:

Growth Mindset Journal

Most positive thing.

CHECKLIST

FELT INSPIRED	☐
ACHIEVED SOMETHING	☐
MADE A MISTAKE	☐
LEARNT SOMETHING NEW	☐
DID A DIFFICULT THING	☐
TRIED SOMETHING NEW	☐
HELPED SOMEONE	☐
SOMEONE HELPED ME	☐
FELT PROUD	☐
SURPRISED MYSELF	☐
TRIED MY BEST	☐
STAYED FOCUSED	☐
IMPROVED A SKILL	☐
PERSONAL BEST	☐
ENJOYED A CHALLENGE	☐
REACHED A GOAL	☐
SET A NEW GOAL	☐
SOLVED A PROBLEM	☐

A challenge you faced.

Say a negative thing in a positive way.

A mistake you made.

What you learned from that mistake.

Set a goal, however big or small.

MINDSET-O-METER

FIXED   GROWTH

Date:

Growth Mindset Journal

Most positive thing.

CHECKLIST

FELT INSPIRED	☐
ACHIEVED SOMETHING	☐
MADE A MISTAKE	☐
LEARNT SOMETHING NEW	☐
DID A DIFFICULT THING	☐
TRIED SOMETHING NEW	☐
HELPED SOMEONE	☐
SOMEONE HELPED ME	☐
FELT PROUD	☐
SURPRISED MYSELF	☐
TRIED MY BEST	☐
STAYED FOCUSED	☐
IMPROVED A SKILL	☐
PERSONAL BEST	☐
ENJOYED A CHALLENGE	☐
REACHED A GOAL	☐
SET A NEW GOAL	☐
SOLVED A PROBLEM	☐

A challenge you faced.

Say a negative thing in a positive way.

A mistake you made.

What you learned from that mistake.

Set a goal, however big or small.

MINDSET-O-METER

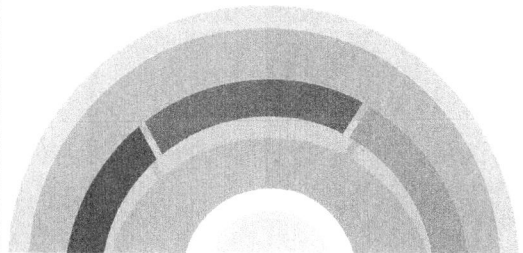

FIXED   **GROWTH**

Date:

Growth Mindset Journal

Most positive thing.

CHECKLIST

FELT INSPIRED	☐
ACHIEVED SOMETHING	☐
MADE A MISTAKE	☐
LEARNT SOMETHING NEW	☐
DID A DIFFICULT THING	☐
TRIED SOMETHING NEW	☐
HELPED SOMEONE	☐
SOMEONE HELPED ME	☐
FELT PROUD	☐
SURPRISED MYSELF	☐
TRIED MY BEST	☐
STAYED FOCUSED	☐
IMPROVED A SKILL	☐
PERSONAL BEST	☐
ENJOYED A CHALLENGE	☐
REACHED A GOAL	☐
SET A NEW GOAL	☐
SOLVED A PROBLEM	☐

A challenge you faced.

Say a negative thing in a positive way.

A mistake you made.

What you learned from that mistake.

Set a goal, however big or small.

MINDSET-O-METER

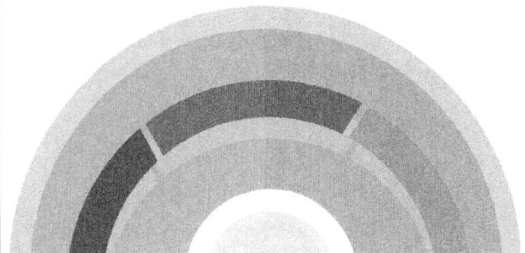

FIXED   GROWTH

Date:

Growth Mindset Journal

Most positive thing.

CHECKLIST

FELT INSPIRED ☐
ACHIEVED SOMETHING ☐
MADE A MISTAKE ☐
LEARNT SOMETHING NEW ☐
DID A DIFFICULT THING ☐
TRIED SOMETHING NEW ☐
HELPED SOMEONE ☐
SOMEONE HELPED ME ☐
FELT PROUD ☐
SURPRISED MYSELF ☐
TRIED MY BEST ☐
STAYED FOCUSED ☐
IMPROVED A SKILL ☐
PERSONAL BEST ☐
ENJOYED A CHALLENGE ☐
REACHED A GOAL ☐
SET A NEW GOAL ☐
SOLVED A PROBLEM ☐

A challenge you faced.

Say a negative thing in a positive way.

A mistake you made.

What you learned from that mistake.

Set a goal, however big or small.

MINDSET-O-METER

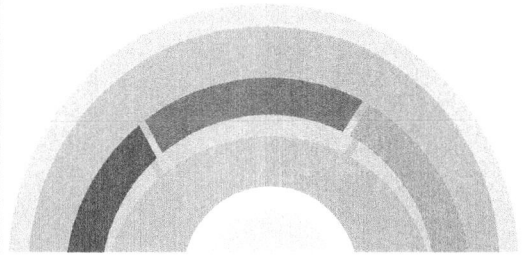

FIXED   GROWTH

Growth Mindset Journal

Most positive thing.

CHECKLIST

FELT INSPIRED ☐
ACHIEVED SOMETHING ☐
MADE A MISTAKE ☐
LEARNT SOMETHING NEW ☐
DID A DIFFICULT THING ☐
TRIED SOMETHING NEW ☐
HELPED SOMEONE ☐
SOMEONE HELPED ME ☐
FELT PROUD ☐
SURPRISED MYSELF ☐
TRIED MY BEST ☐
STAYED FOCUSED ☐
IMPROVED A SKILL ☐
PERSONAL BEST ☐
ENJOYED A CHALLENGE ☐
REACHED A GOAL ☐
SET A NEW GOAL ☐
SOLVED A PROBLEM ☐

A challenge you faced.

Say a negative thing in a positive way.

A mistake you made.

What you learned from that mistake.

Set a goal, however big or small.

MINDSET-O-METER

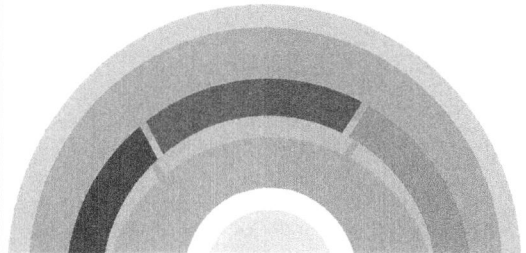

FIXED

GROWTH

Growth Mindset Journal

Most positive thing.

CHECKLIST

FELT INSPIRED	☐
ACHIEVED SOMETHING	☐
MADE A MISTAKE	☐
LEARNT SOMETHING NEW	☐
DID A DIFFICULT THING	☐
TRIED SOMETHING NEW	☐
HELPED SOMEONE	☐
SOMEONE HELPED ME	☐
FELT PROUD	☐
SURPRISED MYSELF	☐
TRIED MY BEST	☐
STAYED FOCUSED	☐
IMPROVED A SKILL	☐
PERSONAL BEST	☐
ENJOYED A CHALLENGE	☐
REACHED A GOAL	☐
SET A NEW GOAL	☐
SOLVED A PROBLEM	☐

A challenge you faced.

Say a negative thing in a positive way.

A mistake you made.

What you learned from that mistake.

Set a goal, however big or small.

MINDSET-O-METER

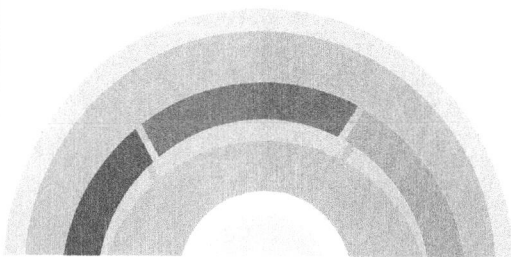

FIXED   GROWTH

Growth Mindset Journal

Date:

Most positive thing.

A challenge you faced.

Say a negative thing in a positive way.

CHECKLIST

FELT INSPIRED ▢
ACHIEVED SOMETHING ▢
MADE A MISTAKE ▢
LEARNT SOMETHING NEW ▢
DID A DIFFICULT THING ▢
TRIED SOMETHING NEW ▢
HELPED SOMEONE ▢
SOMEONE HELPED ME ▢
FELT PROUD ▢
SURPRISED MYSELF ▢
TRIED MY BEST ▢
STAYED FOCUSED ▢
IMPROVED A SKILL ▢
PERSONAL BEST ▢
ENJOYED A CHALLENGE ▢
REACHED A GOAL ▢
SET A NEW GOAL ▢
SOLVED A PROBLEM ▢

A mistake you made.

What you learned from that mistake.

Set a goal, however big or small.

MINDSET-O-METER

FIXED   GROWTH

Growth Mindset Journal

Most positive thing.

CHECKLIST

FELT INSPIRED ☐
ACHIEVED SOMETHING ☐
MADE A MISTAKE ☐
LEARNT SOMETHING NEW ☐
DID A DIFFICULT THING ☐
TRIED SOMETHING NEW ☐
HELPED SOMEONE ☐
SOMEONE HELPED ME ☐
FELT PROUD ☐
SURPRISED MYSELF ☐
TRIED MY BEST ☐
STAYED FOCUSED ☐
IMPROVED A SKILL ☐
PERSONAL BEST ☐
ENJOYED A CHALLENGE ☐
REACHED A GOAL ☐
SET A NEW GOAL ☐
SOLVED A PROBLEM ☐

A challenge you faced.

Say a negative thing in a positive way.

A mistake you made.

What you learned from that mistake.

Set a goal, however big or small.

MINDSET-O-METER

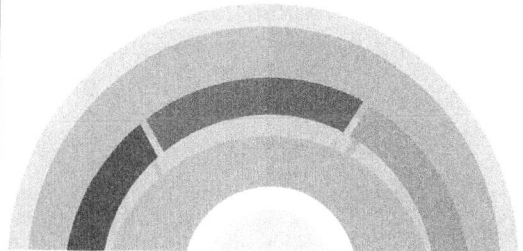

FIXED   GROWTH

Date:

Growth Mindset Journal

Most positive thing.

CHECKLIST

FELT INSPIRED ☐
ACHIEVED SOMETHING ☐
MADE A MISTAKE ☐
LEARNT SOMETHING NEW ☐
DID A DIFFICULT THING ☐
TRIED SOMETHING NEW ☐
HELPED SOMEONE ☐
SOMEONE HELPED ME ☐
FELT PROUD ☐
SURPRISED MYSELF ☐
TRIED MY BEST ☐
STAYED FOCUSED ☐
IMPROVED A SKILL ☐
PERSONAL BEST ☐
ENJOYED A CHALLENGE ☐
REACHED A GOAL ☐
SET A NEW GOAL ☐
SOLVED A PROBLEM ☐

A challenge you faced.

Say a negative thing in a positive way.

A mistake you made.

What you learned from that mistake.

Set a goal, however big or small.

MINDSET-O-METER

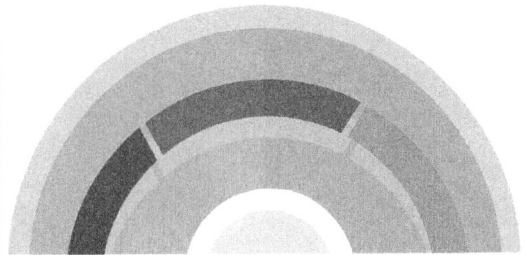

FIXED   GROWTH

Date:

Growth Mindset Journal

Most positive thing.

CHECKLIST

FELT INSPIRED   ☐
ACHIEVED SOMETHING   ☐
MADE A MISTAKE   ☐
LEARNT SOMETHING NEW   ☐
DID A DIFFICULT THING   ☐
TRIED SOMETHING NEW   ☐
HELPED SOMEONE   ☐
SOMEONE HELPED ME   ☐
FELT PROUD   ☐
SURPRISED MYSELF   ☐
TRIED MY BEST   ☐
STAYED FOCUSED   ☐
IMPROVED A SKILL   ☐
PERSONAL BEST   ☐
ENJOYED A CHALLENGE   ☐
REACHED A GOAL   ☐
SET A NEW GOAL   ☐
SOLVED A PROBLEM   ☐

A challenge you faced.

Say a negative thing in a positive way.

A mistake you made.

What you learned from that mistake.

Set a goal, however big or small.

MINDSET-O-METER

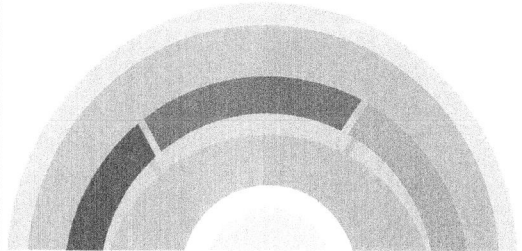

FIXED   GROWTH

Growth Mindset Journal

Most positive thing.

CHECKLIST

FELT INSPIRED	☐
ACHIEVED SOMETHING	☐
MADE A MISTAKE	☐
LEARNT SOMETHING NEW	☐
DID A DIFFICULT THING	☐
TRIED SOMETHING NEW	☐
HELPED SOMEONE	☐
SOMEONE HELPED ME	☐
FELT PROUD	☐
SURPRISED MYSELF	☐
TRIED MY BEST	☐
STAYED FOCUSED	☐
IMPROVED A SKILL	☐
PERSONAL BEST	☐
ENJOYED A CHALLENGE	☐
REACHED A GOAL	☐
SET A NEW GOAL	☐
SOLVED A PROBLEM	☐

A challenge you faced.

Say a negative thing in a positive way.

A mistake you made.

What you learned from that mistake.

Set a goal, however big or small.

MINDSET-O-METER

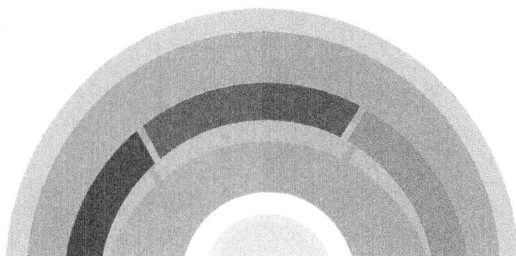

FIXED   GROWTH

Date:

Growth Mindset Journal

Most positive thing.

CHECKLIST

FELT INSPIRED	☐
ACHIEVED SOMETHING	☐
MADE A MISTAKE	☐
LEARNT SOMETHING NEW	☐
DID A DIFFICULT THING	☐
TRIED SOMETHING NEW	☐
HELPED SOMEONE	☐
SOMEONE HELPED ME	☐
FELT PROUD	☐
SURPRISED MYSELF	☐
TRIED MY BEST	☐
STAYED FOCUSED	☐
IMPROVED A SKILL	☐
PERSONAL BEST	☐
ENJOYED A CHALLENGE	☐
REACHED A GOAL	☐
SET A NEW GOAL	☐
SOLVED A PROBLEM	☐

A challenge you faced.

Say a negative thing in a positive way.

A mistake you made.

What you learned from that mistake.

Set a goal, however big or small.

MINDSET-O-METER

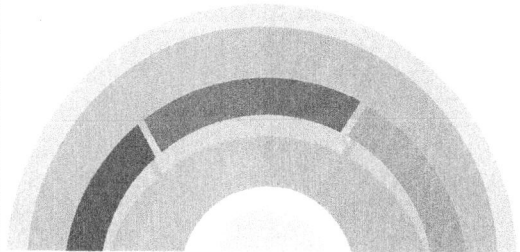

FIXED   GROWTH

Date:

Growth Mindset Journal

Most positive thing.

CHECKLIST

FELT INSPIRED	☐
ACHIEVED SOMETHING	☐
MADE A MISTAKE	☐
LEARNT SOMETHING NEW	☐
DID A DIFFICULT THING	☐
TRIED SOMETHING NEW	☐
HELPED SOMEONE	☐
SOMEONE HELPED ME	☐
FELT PROUD	☐
SURPRISED MYSELF	☐
TRIED MY BEST	☐
STAYED FOCUSED	☐
IMPROVED A SKILL	☐
PERSONAL BEST	☐
ENJOYED A CHALLENGE	☐
REACHED A GOAL	☐
SET A NEW GOAL	☐
SOLVED A PROBLEM	☐

A challenge you faced.

Say a negative thing in a positive way.

A mistake you made.

What you learned from that mistake.

Set a goal, however big or small.

MINDSET-O-METER

FIXED   GROWTH

Date:

Growth Mindset Journal

Most positive thing.

CHECKLIST

FELT INSPIRED ☐
ACHIEVED SOMETHING ☐
MADE A MISTAKE ☐
LEARNT SOMETHING NEW ☐
DID A DIFFICULT THING ☐
TRIED SOMETHING NEW ☐
HELPED SOMEONE ☐
SOMEONE HELPED ME ☐
FELT PROUD ☐
SURPRISED MYSELF ☐
TRIED MY BEST ☐
STAYED FOCUSED ☐
IMPROVED A SKILL ☐
PERSONAL BEST ☐
ENJOYED A CHALLENGE ☐
REACHED A GOAL ☐
SET A NEW GOAL ☐
SOLVED A PROBLEM ☐

A challenge you faced.

Say a negative thing in a positive way.

A mistake you made.

What you learned from that mistake.

Set a goal, however big or small.

MINDSET-O-METER

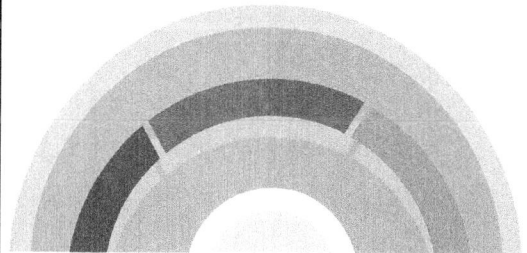

FIXED   GROWTH

Growth Mindset Journal

Most positive thing.

CHECKLIST

FELT INSPIRED	☐
ACHIEVED SOMETHING	☐
MADE A MISTAKE	☐
LEARNT SOMETHING NEW	☐
DID A DIFFICULT THING	☐
TRIED SOMETHING NEW	☐
HELPED SOMEONE	☐
SOMEONE HELPED ME	☐
FELT PROUD	☐
SURPRISED MYSELF	☐
TRIED MY BEST	☐
STAYED FOCUSED	☐
IMPROVED A SKILL	☐
PERSONAL BEST	☐
ENJOYED A CHALLENGE	☐
REACHED A GOAL	☐
SET A NEW GOAL	☐
SOLVED A PROBLEM	☐

A challenge you faced.

Say a negative thing in a positive way.

A mistake you made.

What you learned from that mistake.

Set a goal, however big or small.

MINDSET-O-METER

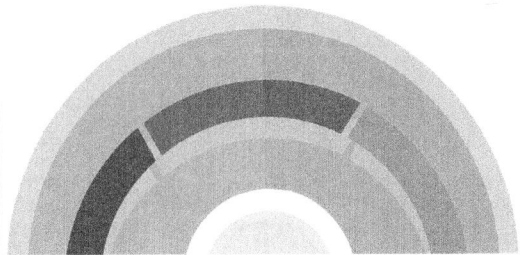

FIXED   GROWTH

Date:

Growth Mindset Journal

Most positive thing.

A challenge you faced.

Say a negative thing in a positive way.

CHECKLIST

FELT INSPIRED	☐
ACHIEVED SOMETHING	☐
MADE A MISTAKE	☐
LEARNT SOMETHING NEW	☐
DID A DIFFICULT THING	☐
TRIED SOMETHING NEW	☐
HELPED SOMEONE	☐
SOMEONE HELPED ME	☐
FELT PROUD	☐
SURPRISED MYSELF	☐
TRIED MY BEST	☐
STAYED FOCUSED	☐
IMPROVED A SKILL	☐
PERSONAL BEST	☐
ENJOYED A CHALLENGE	☐
REACHED A GOAL	☐
SET A NEW GOAL	☐
SOLVED A PROBLEM	☐

A mistake you made.

What you learned from that mistake.

Set a goal, however big or small.

MINDSET-O-METER

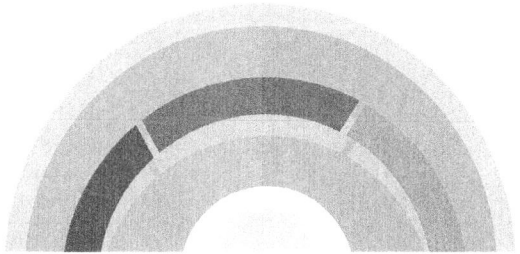

FIXED   GROWTH

Growth Mindset Journal

Most positive thing.

CHECKLIST

FELT INSPIRED	☐
ACHIEVED SOMETHING	☐
MADE A MISTAKE	☐
LEARNT SOMETHING NEW	☐
DID A DIFFICULT THING	☐
TRIED SOMETHING NEW	☐
HELPED SOMEONE	☐
SOMEONE HELPED ME	☐
FELT PROUD	☐
SURPRISED MYSELF	☐
TRIED MY BEST	☐
STAYED FOCUSED	☐
IMPROVED A SKILL	☐
PERSONAL BEST	☐
ENJOYED A CHALLENGE	☐
REACHED A GOAL	☐
SET A NEW GOAL	☐
SOLVED A PROBLEM	☐

A challenge you faced.

Say a negative thing in a positive way.

A mistake you made.

What you learned from that mistake.

Set a goal, however big or small.

MINDSET-O-METER

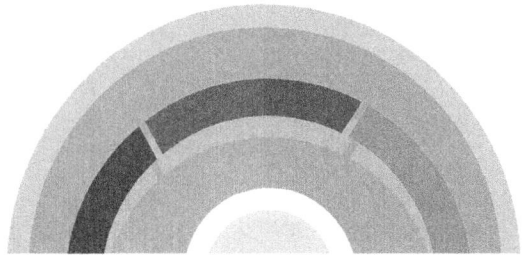

FIXED

GROWTH

Growth Mindset Journal

Most positive thing.

CHECKLIST

FELT INSPIRED ☐
ACHIEVED SOMETHING ☐
MADE A MISTAKE ☐
LEARNT SOMETHING NEW ☐
DID A DIFFICULT THING ☐
TRIED SOMETHING NEW ☐
HELPED SOMEONE ☐
SOMEONE HELPED ME ☐
FELT PROUD ☐
SURPRISED MYSELF ☐
TRIED MY BEST ☐
STAYED FOCUSED ☐
IMPROVED A SKILL ☐
PERSONAL BEST ☐
ENJOYED A CHALLENGE ☐
REACHED A GOAL ☐
SET A NEW GOAL ☐
SOLVED A PROBLEM ☐

A challenge you faced.

Say a negative thing in a positive way.

A mistake you made.

What you learned from that mistake.

Set a goal, however big or small.

MINDSET-O-METER

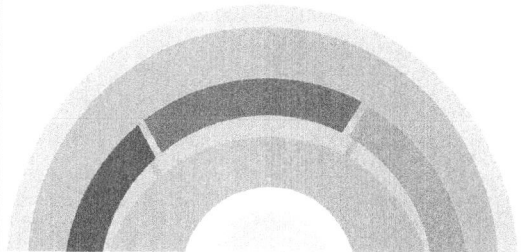

FIXED   GROWTH

Date:

Growth Mindset Journal

Most positive thing.

CHECKLIST

FELT INSPIRED ☐
ACHIEVED SOMETHING ☐
MADE A MISTAKE ☐
LEARNT SOMETHING NEW ☐
DID A DIFFICULT THING ☐
TRIED SOMETHING NEW ☐
HELPED SOMEONE ☐
SOMEONE HELPED ME ☐
FELT PROUD ☐
SURPRISED MYSELF ☐
TRIED MY BEST ☐
STAYED FOCUSED ☐
IMPROVED A SKILL ☐
PERSONAL BEST ☐
ENJOYED A CHALLENGE ☐
REACHED A GOAL ☐
SET A NEW GOAL ☐
SOLVED A PROBLEM ☐

A challenge you faced.

Say a negative thing in a positive way.

A mistake you made.

What you learned from that mistake.

Set a goal, however big or small.

MINDSET-O-METER

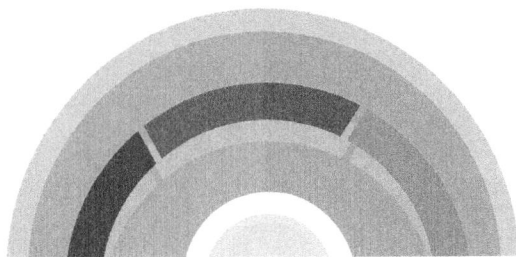

FIXED   GROWTH

Growth Mindset Journal

Most positive thing.

CHECKLIST

FELT INSPIRED ▫
ACHIEVED SOMETHING ▫
MADE A MISTAKE ▫
LEARNT SOMETHING NEW ▫
DID A DIFFICULT THING ▫
TRIED SOMETHING NEW ▫
HELPED SOMEONE ▫
SOMEONE HELPED ME ▫
FELT PROUD ▫
SURPRISED MYSELF ▫
TRIED MY BEST ▫
STAYED FOCUSED ▫
IMPROVED A SKILL ▫
PERSONAL BEST ▫
ENJOYED A CHALLENGE ▫
REACHED A GOAL ▫
SET A NEW GOAL ▫
SOLVED A PROBLEM ▫

A challenge you faced.

Say a negative thing in a positive way.

A mistake you made.

What you learned from that mistake.

Set a goal, however big or small.

MINDSET-O-METER

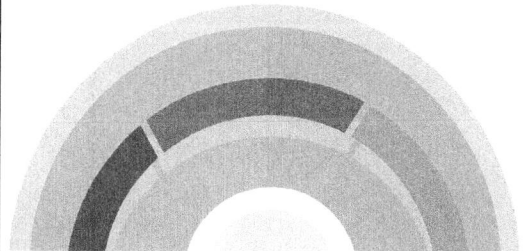

FIXED   GROWTH

Date:

Growth Mindset Journal

Most positive thing.

CHECKLIST

FELT INSPIRED	☐
ACHIEVED SOMETHING	☐
MADE A MISTAKE	☐
LEARNT SOMETHING NEW	☐
DID A DIFFICULT THING	☐
TRIED SOMETHING NEW	☐
HELPED SOMEONE	☐
SOMEONE HELPED ME	☐
FELT PROUD	☐
SURPRISED MYSELF	☐
TRIED MY BEST	☐
STAYED FOCUSED	☐
IMPROVED A SKILL	☐
PERSONAL BEST	☐
ENJOYED A CHALLENGE	☐
REACHED A GOAL	☐
SET A NEW GOAL	☐
SOLVED A PROBLEM	☐

A challenge you faced.

Say a negative thing in a positive way.

A mistake you made.

What you learned from that mistake.

Set a goal, however big or small.

MINDSET-O-METER

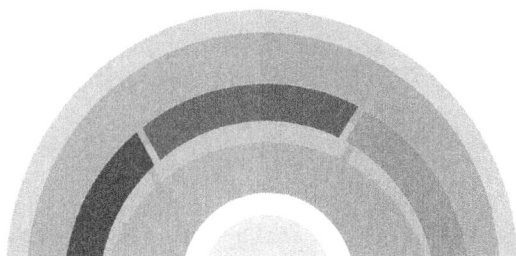

FIXED   GROWTH

Date:

Growth Mindset Journal

Most positive thing.

A challenge you faced.

Say a negative thing in a positive way.

CHECKLIST

FELT INSPIRED ☐
ACHIEVED SOMETHING ☐
MADE A MISTAKE ☐
LEARNT SOMETHING NEW ☐
DID A DIFFICULT THING ☐
TRIED SOMETHING NEW ☐
HELPED SOMEONE ☐
SOMEONE HELPED ME ☐
FELT PROUD ☐
SURPRISED MYSELF ☐
TRIED MY BEST ☐
STAYED FOCUSED ☐
IMPROVED A SKILL ☐
PERSONAL BEST ☐
ENJOYED A CHALLENGE ☐
REACHED A GOAL ☐
SET A NEW GOAL ☐
SOLVED A PROBLEM ☐

A mistake you made.

What you learned from that mistake.

Set a goal, however big or small.

MINDSET-O-METER

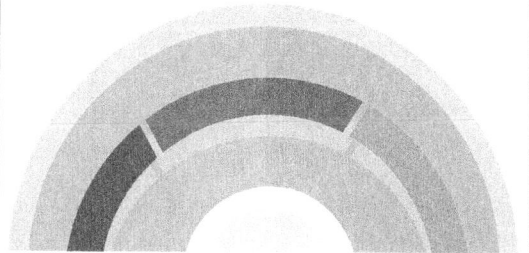

FIXED   GROWTH

Growth Mindset Journal

Most positive thing.

CHECKLIST

FELT INSPIRED	▢
ACHIEVED SOMETHING	▢
MADE A MISTAKE	▢
LEARNT SOMETHING NEW	▢
DID A DIFFICULT THING	▢
TRIED SOMETHING NEW	▢
HELPED SOMEONE	▢
SOMEONE HELPED ME	▢
FELT PROUD	▢
SURPRISED MYSELF	▢
TRIED MY BEST	▢
STAYED FOCUSED	▢
IMPROVED A SKILL	▢
PERSONAL BEST	▢
ENJOYED A CHALLENGE	▢
REACHED A GOAL	▢
SET A NEW GOAL	▢
SOLVED A PROBLEM	▢

A challenge you faced.

Say a negative thing in a positive way.

A mistake you made.

What you learned from that mistake.

Set a goal, however big or small.

MINDSET-O-METER

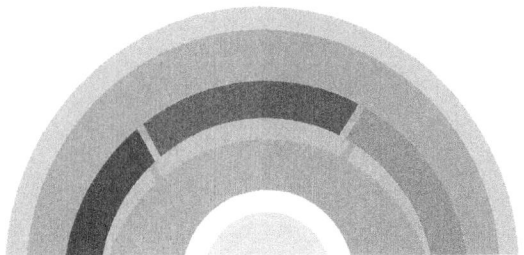

FIXED   GROWTH

Date:

Growth Mindset Journal

Most positive thing.

CHECKLIST

FELT INSPIRED	☐
ACHIEVED SOMETHING	☐
MADE A MISTAKE	☐
LEARNT SOMETHING NEW	☐
DID A DIFFICULT THING	☐
TRIED SOMETHING NEW	☐
HELPED SOMEONE	☐
SOMEONE HELPED ME	☐
FELT PROUD	☐
SURPRISED MYSELF	☐
TRIED MY BEST	☐
STAYED FOCUSED	☐
IMPROVED A SKILL	☐
PERSONAL BEST	☐
ENJOYED A CHALLENGE	☐
REACHED A GOAL	☐
SET A NEW GOAL	☐
SOLVED A PROBLEM	☐

A challenge you faced.

Say a negative thing in a positive way.

A mistake you made.

What you learned from that mistake.

Set a goal, however big or small.

MINDSET-O-METER

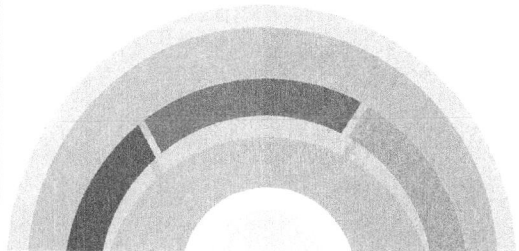

FIXED   GROWTH

Growth Mindset Journal

Most positive thing.

CHECKLIST

FELT INSPIRED ☐
ACHIEVED SOMETHING ☐
MADE A MISTAKE ☐
LEARNT SOMETHING NEW ☐
DID A DIFFICULT THING ☐
TRIED SOMETHING NEW ☐
HELPED SOMEONE ☐
SOMEONE HELPED ME ☐
FELT PROUD ☐
SURPRISED MYSELF ☐
TRIED MY BEST ☐
STAYED FOCUSED ☐
IMPROVED A SKILL ☐
PERSONAL BEST ☐
ENJOYED A CHALLENGE ☐
REACHED A GOAL ☐
SET A NEW GOAL ☐
SOLVED A PROBLEM ☐

A challenge you faced.

Say a negative thing in a positive way.

A mistake you made.

What you learned from that mistake.

Set a goal, however big or small.

MINDSET-O-METER

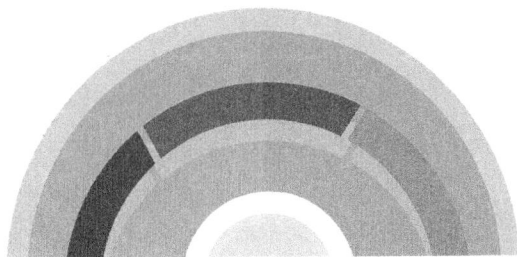

FIXED   GROWTH

Growth Mindset Journal

Date:

Most positive thing.

A challenge you faced.

Say a negative thing in a positive way.

CHECKLIST

FELT INSPIRED ☐
ACHIEVED SOMETHING ☐
MADE A MISTAKE ☐
LEARNT SOMETHING NEW ☐
DID A DIFFICULT THING ☐
TRIED SOMETHING NEW ☐
HELPED SOMEONE ☐
SOMEONE HELPED ME ☐
FELT PROUD ☐
SURPRISED MYSELF ☐
TRIED MY BEST ☐
STAYED FOCUSED ☐
IMPROVED A SKILL ☐
PERSONAL BEST ☐
ENJOYED A CHALLENGE ☐
REACHED A GOAL ☐
SET A NEW GOAL ☐
SOLVED A PROBLEM ☐

A mistake you made.

What you learned from that mistake.

Set a goal, however big or small.

MINDSET-O-METER

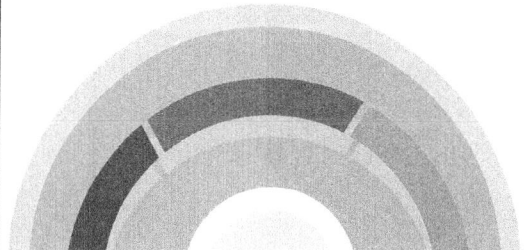

FIXED   GROWTH

Date:

Growth Mindset Journal

Most positive thing.

CHECKLIST

FELT INSPIRED ☐
ACHIEVED SOMETHING ☐
MADE A MISTAKE ☐
LEARNT SOMETHING NEW ☐
DID A DIFFICULT THING ☐
TRIED SOMETHING NEW ☐
HELPED SOMEONE ☐
SOMEONE HELPED ME ☐
FELT PROUD ☐
SURPRISED MYSELF ☐
TRIED MY BEST ☐
STAYED FOCUSED ☐
IMPROVED A SKILL ☐
PERSONAL BEST ☐
ENJOYED A CHALLENGE ☐
REACHED A GOAL ☐
SET A NEW GOAL ☐
SOLVED A PROBLEM ☐

A challenge you faced.

Say a negative thing in a positive way.

A mistake you made.

What you learned from that mistake.

Set a goal, however big or small.

MINDSET-O-METER

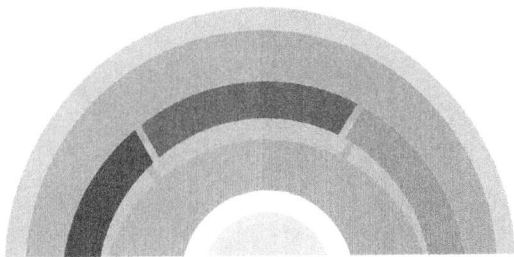

FIXED   GROWTH

Growth Mindset Journal

Most positive thing.

CHECKLIST

FELT INSPIRED ☐
ACHIEVED SOMETHING ☐
MADE A MISTAKE ☐
LEARNT SOMETHING NEW ☐
DID A DIFFICULT THING ☐
TRIED SOMETHING NEW ☐
HELPED SOMEONE ☐
SOMEONE HELPED ME ☐
FELT PROUD ☐
SURPRISED MYSELF ☐
TRIED MY BEST ☐
STAYED FOCUSED ☐
IMPROVED A SKILL ☐
PERSONAL BEST ☐
ENJOYED A CHALLENGE ☐
REACHED A GOAL ☐
SET A NEW GOAL ☐
SOLVED A PROBLEM ☐

A challenge you faced.

Say a negative thing in a positive way.

A mistake you made.

What you learned from that mistake.

Set a goal, however big or small.

MINDSET-O-METER

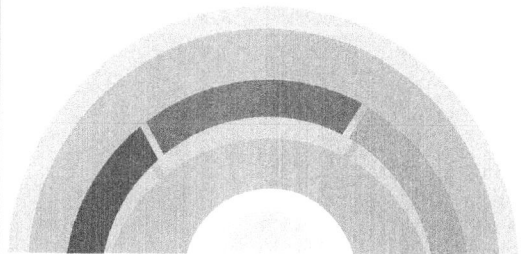

FIXED   GROWTH

Growth Mindset Journal

Most positive thing.

CHECKLIST

FELT INSPIRED ☐
ACHIEVED SOMETHING ☐
MADE A MISTAKE ☐
LEARNT SOMETHING NEW ☐
DID A DIFFICULT THING ☐
TRIED SOMETHING NEW ☐
HELPED SOMEONE ☐
SOMEONE HELPED ME ☐
FELT PROUD ☐
SURPRISED MYSELF ☐
TRIED MY BEST ☐
STAYED FOCUSED ☐
IMPROVED A SKILL ☐
PERSONAL BEST ☐
ENJOYED A CHALLENGE ☐
REACHED A GOAL ☐
SET A NEW GOAL ☐
SOLVED A PROBLEM ☐

A challenge you faced.

Say a negative thing in a positive way.

A mistake you made.

What you learned from that mistake.

Set a goal, however big or small.

MINDSET-O-METER

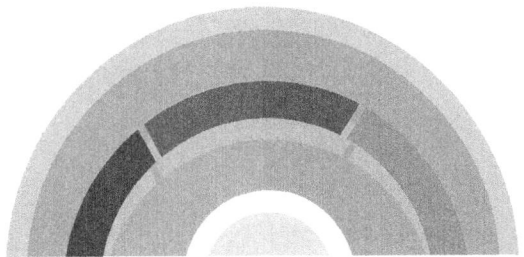

FIXED   GROWTH

Growth Mindset Journal

Date:

Most positive thing.

A challenge you faced.

Say a negative thing in a positive way.

CHECKLIST

FELT INSPIRED ☐
ACHIEVED SOMETHING ☐
MADE A MISTAKE ☐
LEARNT SOMETHING NEW ☐
DID A DIFFICULT THING ☐
TRIED SOMETHING NEW ☐
HELPED SOMEONE ☐
SOMEONE HELPED ME ☐
FELT PROUD ☐
SURPRISED MYSELF ☐
TRIED MY BEST ☐
STAYED FOCUSED ☐
IMPROVED A SKILL ☐
PERSONAL BEST ☐
ENJOYED A CHALLENGE ☐
REACHED A GOAL ☐
SET A NEW GOAL ☐
SOLVED A PROBLEM ☐

A mistake you made.

What you learned from that mistake.

Set a goal, however big or small.

MINDSET-O-METER

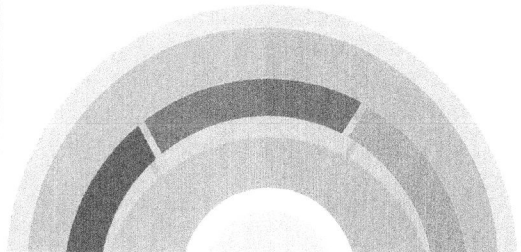

FIXED   GROWTH

Date:

Growth Mindset Journal

Most positive thing.

CHECKLIST

FELT INSPIRED   ☐
ACHIEVED SOMETHING   ☐
MADE A MISTAKE   ☐
LEARNT SOMETHING NEW   ☐
DID A DIFFICULT THING   ☐
TRIED SOMETHING NEW   ☐
HELPED SOMEONE   ☐
SOMEONE HELPED ME   ☐
FELT PROUD   ☐
SURPRISED MYSELF   ☐
TRIED MY BEST   ☐
STAYED FOCUSED   ☐
IMPROVED A SKILL   ☐
PERSONAL BEST   ☐
ENJOYED A CHALLENGE   ☐
REACHED A GOAL   ☐
SET A NEW GOAL   ☐
SOLVED A PROBLEM   ☐

A challenge you faced.

Say a negative thing in a positive way.

A mistake you made.

What you learned from that mistake.

Set a goal, however big or small.

MINDSET-O-METER

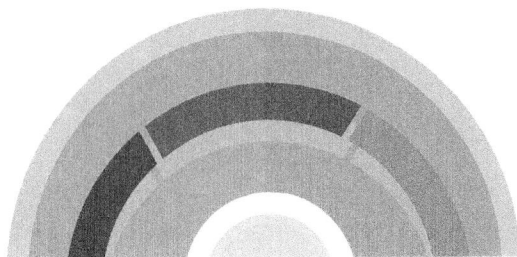

FIXED   GROWTH

Growth Mindset Journal

Most positive thing.

CHECKLIST

FELT INSPIRED ☐
ACHIEVED SOMETHING ☐
MADE A MISTAKE ☐
LEARNT SOMETHING NEW ☐
DID A DIFFICULT THING ☐
TRIED SOMETHING NEW ☐
HELPED SOMEONE ☐
SOMEONE HELPED ME ☐
FELT PROUD ☐
SURPRISED MYSELF ☐
TRIED MY BEST ☐
STAYED FOCUSED ☐
IMPROVED A SKILL ☐
PERSONAL BEST ☐
ENJOYED A CHALLENGE ☐
REACHED A GOAL ☐
SET A NEW GOAL ☐
SOLVED A PROBLEM ☐

A challenge you faced.

Say a negative thing in a positive way.

A mistake you made.

What you learned from that mistake.

Set a goal, however big or small.

MINDSET-O-METER

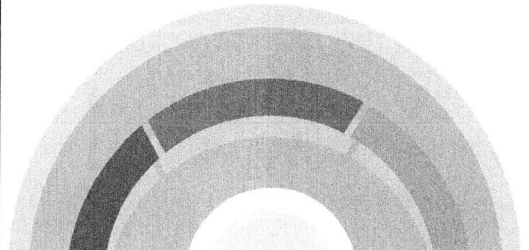

FIXED   **GROWTH**

Growth Mindset Journal

Date:

Most positive thing.

A challenge you faced.

Say a negative thing in a positive way.

CHECKLIST

FELT INSPIRED	☐
ACHIEVED SOMETHING	☐
MADE A MISTAKE	☐
LEARNT SOMETHING NEW	☐
DID A DIFFICULT THING	☐
TRIED SOMETHING NEW	☐
HELPED SOMEONE	☐
SOMEONE HELPED ME	☐
FELT PROUD	☐
SURPRISED MYSELF	☐
TRIED MY BEST	☐
STAYED FOCUSED	☐
IMPROVED A SKILL	☐
PERSONAL BEST	☐
ENJOYED A CHALLENGE	☐
REACHED A GOAL	☐
SET A NEW GOAL	☐
SOLVED A PROBLEM	☐

A mistake you made.

What you learned from that mistake.

Set a goal, however big or small.

MINDSET-O-METER

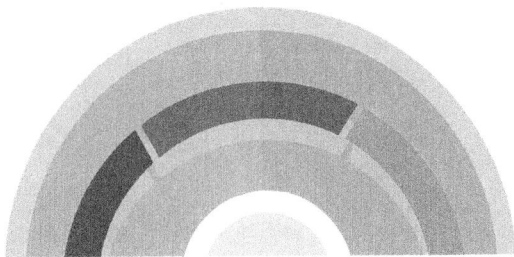

FIXED   GROWTH

Date:

Growth Mindset Journal

Most positive thing.

CHECKLIST

FELT INSPIRED ☐
ACHIEVED SOMETHING ☐
MADE A MISTAKE ☐
LEARNT SOMETHING NEW ☐
DID A DIFFICULT THING ☐
TRIED SOMETHING NEW ☐
HELPED SOMEONE ☐
SOMEONE HELPED ME ☐
FELT PROUD ☐
SURPRISED MYSELF ☐
TRIED MY BEST ☐
STAYED FOCUSED ☐
IMPROVED A SKILL ☐
PERSONAL BEST ☐
ENJOYED A CHALLENGE ☐
REACHED A GOAL ☐
SET A NEW GOAL ☐
SOLVED A PROBLEM ☐

A challenge you faced.

Say a negative thing in a positive way.

A mistake you made.

What you learned from that mistake.

Set a goal, however big or small.

MINDSET-O-METER

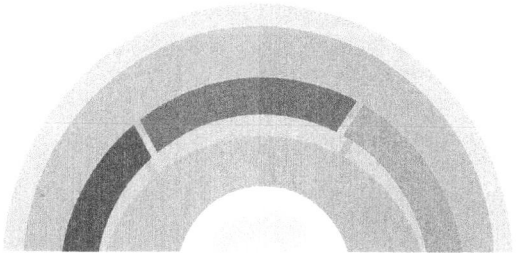

FIXED   GROWTH

Growth Mindset Journal

Most positive thing.

FELT INSPIRED   ☐
ACHIEVED SOMETHING   ☐
MADE A MISTAKE   ☐
LEARNT SOMETHING NEW   ☐
DID A DIFFICULT THING   ☐
TRIED SOMETHING NEW   ☐
HELPED SOMEONE   ☐
SOMEONE HELPED ME   ☐
FELT PROUD   ☐
SURPRISED MYSELF   ☐
TRIED MY BEST   ☐
STAYED FOCUSED   ☐
IMPROVED A SKILL   ☐
PERSONAL BEST   ☐
ENJOYED A CHALLENGE   ☐
REACHED A GOAL   ☐
SET A NEW GOAL   ☐
SOLVED A PROBLEM   ☐

A challenge you faced.

Say a negative thing in a positive way.

A mistake you made.

What you learned from that mistake.

Set a goal, however big or small.

MINDSET-O-METER

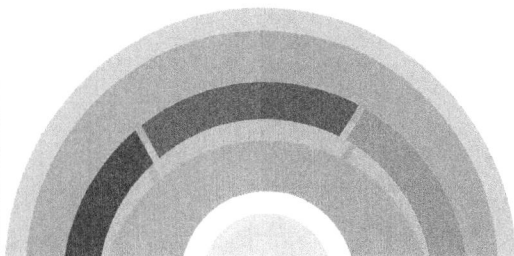

FIXED   GROWTH

Date:

Growth Mindset Journal

Most positive thing.

CHECKLIST

FELT INSPIRED ☐
ACHIEVED SOMETHING ☐
MADE A MISTAKE ☐
LEARNT SOMETHING NEW ☐
DID A DIFFICULT THING ☐
TRIED SOMETHING NEW ☐
HELPED SOMEONE ☐
SOMEONE HELPED ME ☐
FELT PROUD ☐
SURPRISED MYSELF ☐
TRIED MY BEST ☐
STAYED FOCUSED ☐
IMPROVED A SKILL ☐
PERSONAL BEST ☐
ENJOYED A CHALLENGE ☐
REACHED A GOAL ☐
SET A NEW GOAL ☐
SOLVED A PROBLEM ☐

A challenge you faced.

Say a negative thing in a positive way.

A mistake you made.

What you learned from that mistake.

Set a goal, however big or small.

MINDSET-O-METER

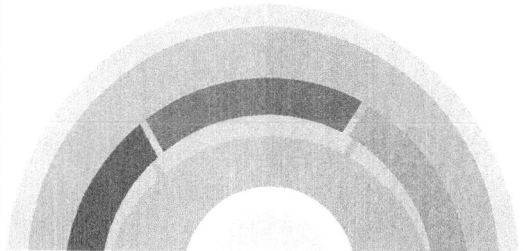

FIXED   GROWTH

Date:

Growth Mindset Journal

Most positive thing.

A challenge you faced.

Say a negative thing in a positive way.

CHECKLIST

FELT INSPIRED	☐
ACHIEVED SOMETHING	☐
MADE A MISTAKE	☐
LEARNT SOMETHING NEW	☐
DID A DIFFICULT THING	☐
TRIED SOMETHING NEW	☐
HELPED SOMEONE	☐
SOMEONE HELPED ME	☐
FELT PROUD	☐
SURPRISED MYSELF	☐
TRIED MY BEST	☐
STAYED FOCUSED	☐
IMPROVED A SKILL	☐
PERSONAL BEST	☐
ENJOYED A CHALLENGE	☐
REACHED A GOAL	☐
SET A NEW GOAL	☐
SOLVED A PROBLEM	☐

A mistake you made.

What you learned from that mistake.

Set a goal, however big or small.

MINDSET-O-METER

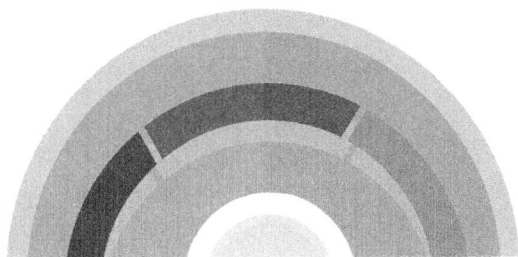

FIXED   GROWTH

Growth Mindset Journal

Most positive thing.

CHECKLIST

FELT INSPIRED	☐
ACHIEVED SOMETHING	☐
MADE A MISTAKE	☐
LEARNT SOMETHING NEW	☐
DID A DIFFICULT THING	☐
TRIED SOMETHING NEW	☐
HELPED SOMEONE	☐
SOMEONE HELPED ME	☐
FELT PROUD	☐
SURPRISED MYSELF	☐
TRIED MY BEST	☐
STAYED FOCUSED	☐
IMPROVED A SKILL	☐
PERSONAL BEST	☐
ENJOYED A CHALLENGE	☐
REACHED A GOAL	☐
SET A NEW GOAL	☐
SOLVED A PROBLEM	☐

A challenge you faced.

Say a negative thing in a positive way.

A mistake you made.

What you learned from that mistake.

Set a goal, however big or small.

MINDSET-O-METER

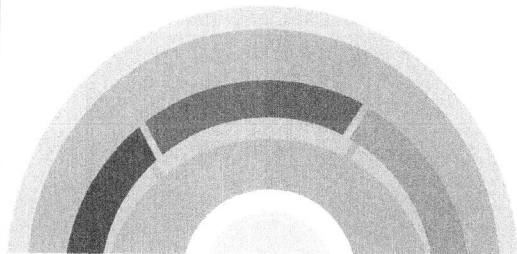

FIXED   GROWTH

Growth Mindset Journal

Most positive thing.

CHECKLIST

FELT INSPIRED	☐
ACHIEVED SOMETHING	☐
MADE A MISTAKE	☐
LEARNT SOMETHING NEW	☐
DID A DIFFICULT THING	☐
TRIED SOMETHING NEW	☐
HELPED SOMEONE	☐
SOMEONE HELPED ME	☐
FELT PROUD	☐
SURPRISED MYSELF	☐
TRIED MY BEST	☐
STAYED FOCUSED	☐
IMPROVED A SKILL	☐
PERSONAL BEST	☐
ENJOYED A CHALLENGE	☐
REACHED A GOAL	☐
SET A NEW GOAL	☐
SOLVED A PROBLEM	☐

A challenge you faced.

Say a negative thing in a positive way.

A mistake you made.

What you learned from that mistake.

Set a goal, however big or small.

MINDSET-O-METER

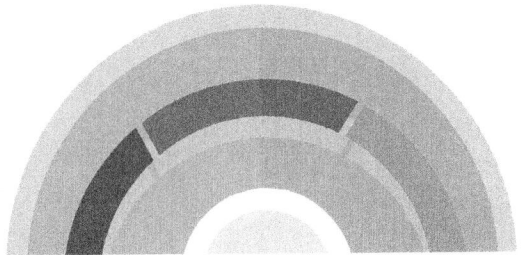

FIXED   GROWTH

Date:

Growth Mindset Journal

Most positive thing.

CHECKLIST

FELT INSPIRED ☐
ACHIEVED SOMETHING ☐
MADE A MISTAKE ☐
LEARNT SOMETHING NEW ☐
DID A DIFFICULT THING ☐
TRIED SOMETHING NEW ☐
HELPED SOMEONE ☐
SOMEONE HELPED ME ☐
FELT PROUD ☐
SURPRISED MYSELF ☐
TRIED MY BEST ☐
STAYED FOCUSED ☐
IMPROVED A SKILL ☐
PERSONAL BEST ☐
ENJOYED A CHALLENGE ☐
REACHED A GOAL ☐
SET A NEW GOAL ☐
SOLVED A PROBLEM ☐

A challenge you faced.

Say a negative thing in a positive way.

A mistake you made.

What you learned from that mistake.

Set a goal, however big or small.

MINDSET-O-METER

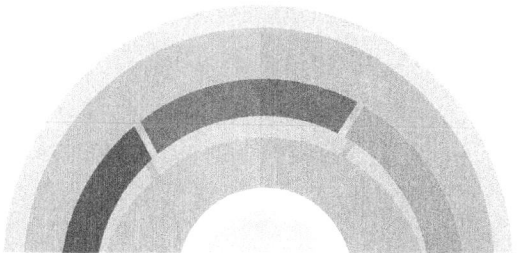

FIXED   GROWTH

Growth Mindset Journal

Most positive thing.

CHECKLIST

FELT INSPIRED ☐
ACHIEVED SOMETHING ☐
MADE A MISTAKE ☐
LEARNT SOMETHING NEW ☐
DID A DIFFICULT THING ☐
TRIED SOMETHING NEW ☐
HELPED SOMEONE ☐
SOMEONE HELPED ME ☐
FELT PROUD ☐
SURPRISED MYSELF ☐
TRIED MY BEST ☐
STAYED FOCUSED ☐
IMPROVED A SKILL ☐
PERSONAL BEST ☐
ENJOYED A CHALLENGE ☐
REACHED A GOAL ☐
SET A NEW GOAL ☐
SOLVED A PROBLEM ☐

A challenge you faced.

Say a negative thing in a positive way.

A mistake you made.

What you learned from that mistake.

Set a goal, however big or small.

MINDSET-O-METER

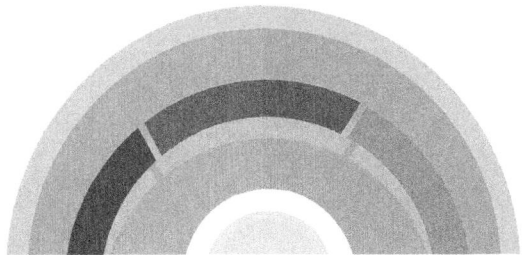

FIXED   GROWTH

Growth Mindset Journal

Most positive thing.

CHECKLIST

FELT INSPIRED ☐
ACHIEVED SOMETHING ☐
MADE A MISTAKE ☐
LEARNT SOMETHING NEW ☐
DID A DIFFICULT THING ☐
TRIED SOMETHING NEW ☐
HELPED SOMEONE ☐
SOMEONE HELPED ME ☐
FELT PROUD ☐
SURPRISED MYSELF ☐
TRIED MY BEST ☐
STAYED FOCUSED ☐
IMPROVED A SKILL ☐
PERSONAL BEST ☐
ENJOYED A CHALLENGE ☐
REACHED A GOAL ☐
SET A NEW GOAL ☐
SOLVED A PROBLEM ☐

A challenge you faced.

Say a negative thing in a positive way.

A mistake you made.

What you learned from that mistake.

Set a goal, however big or small.

MINDSET-O-METER

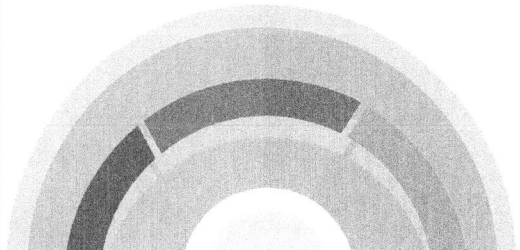

FIXED   GROWTH

Date:

Growth Mindset Journal

Most positive thing.

A challenge you faced.

Say a negative thing in a positive way.

CHECKLIST

FELT INSPIRED	☐
ACHIEVED SOMETHING	☐
MADE A MISTAKE	☐
LEARNT SOMETHING NEW	☐
DID A DIFFICULT THING	☐
TRIED SOMETHING NEW	☐
HELPED SOMEONE	☐
SOMEONE HELPED ME	☐
FELT PROUD	☐
SURPRISED MYSELF	☐
TRIED MY BEST	☐
STAYED FOCUSED	☐
IMPROVED A SKILL	☐
PERSONAL BEST	☐
ENJOYED A CHALLENGE	☐
REACHED A GOAL	☐
SET A NEW GOAL	☐
SOLVED A PROBLEM	☐

A mistake you made.

What you learned from that mistake.

Set a goal, however big or small.

MINDSET-O-METER

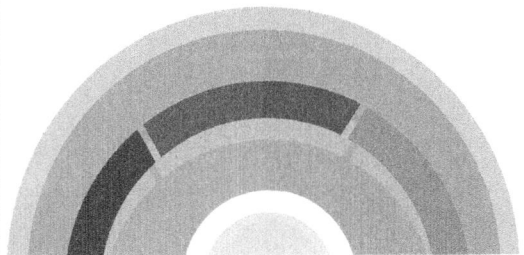

FIXED   GROWTH

Growth Mindset Journal

Most positive thing.

CHECKLIST

FELT INSPIRED	☐
ACHIEVED SOMETHING	☐
MADE A MISTAKE	☐
LEARNT SOMETHING NEW	☐
DID A DIFFICULT THING	☐
TRIED SOMETHING NEW	☐
HELPED SOMEONE	☐
SOMEONE HELPED ME	☐
FELT PROUD	☐
SURPRISED MYSELF	☐
TRIED MY BEST	☐
STAYED FOCUSED	☐
IMPROVED A SKILL	☐
PERSONAL BEST	☐
ENJOYED A CHALLENGE	☐
REACHED A GOAL	☐
SET A NEW GOAL	☐
SOLVED A PROBLEM	☐

A challenge you faced.

Say a negative thing in a positive way.

A mistake you made.

What you learned from that mistake.

Set a goal, however big or small.

MINDSET-O-METER

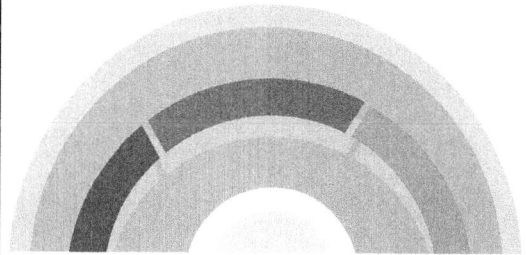

FIXED   GROWTH

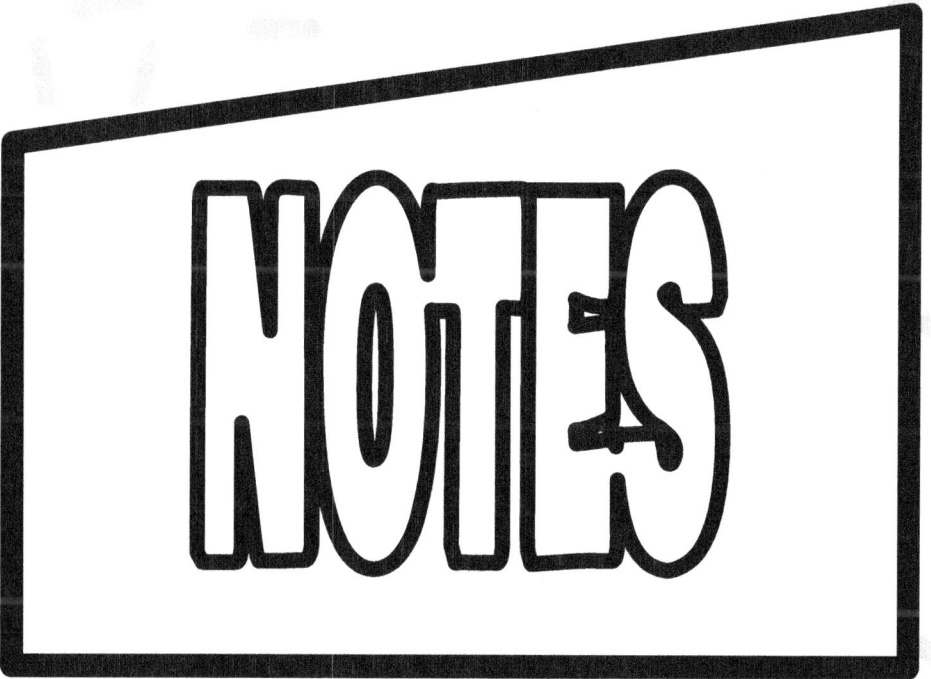

Notes

Notes

Notes

Notes

Notes

Notes

Notes

Notes

Notes

Notes

Notes

Notes

About the guy who made this book

Del Huffman is a Primary School Teacher from the United Kingdom. His career has spanned 3 decades working with children across the globe. He has worked in all sorts of schools but has spent most of his time working with struggling or reluctant learners in SEND (special educational needs and disability) and SEMH (social emotional and mental health needs) settings.

Del worked alongside various specialists like psychologists and therapists on many projects and initiatives to develop forward thinking and effective approaches to engaging and teaching the hardest to reach learners.

Nowadays Del spends his time outside of the classroom creating books and resources to help children learn and manage everyday situations.

Printed in Great Britain
by Amazon